Acting on Faith
Volume 1
Charles M. Tanner

Abingdon Press
Nashville

ACTING ON FAITH

Volume 1

Copyright © 1994 by Charles M. Tanner

94 95 96 97 98 99 00 01 02 03—10 9 8 7 6 5 4 3 2 1

This book is printed on acid-free, recycled paper.

ISBN 0-687-09752-5

MANUFACTURED IN THE UNITED STATES OF AMERICA

CONTENTS

INTRODUCTION

Not only is drama a powerful means of communication, but when it is written thoughtfully along sound theological lines based on the New Testament, it can change—and has changed—people's lives. It is a valuable tool that has a firm place in the teaching, nurturing, and witnessing place in the life of the church.

Perhaps at no time in history has there been a greater need or a more ready atmosphere for drama on the part of congregations and audiences than at present. We are flooded with dramatic material on television, the movies and stage presentations from schools, universities, theaters—from community productions to Broadway itself. More people are witting and knowledgeable of the many elements of theatre today than ever before. And church people are, of course, among those who are aware of these media—presenting, therefore, congregations (audiences) prepared for impact and challenge.

The use of drama in the church has increased apace with the growth of understanding and appreciation of theatre as something more than an entertainment vehicle and/or art form. The impact of films during the golden age of Hollywood is well known to social scientists and has been credited with the overall leveling of the strata in American society from the poor to the very rich. Those films improved confidence, the sense of taste, and methods of speech of those who were exposed to them. Drama, presented live and done well, has an even greater effectiveness capability due to the vitality and vibrancy of the sights and sounds and propinquity of the performers as they project personalities, character and challenges in the very presence of the audience.

Every church should have a drama group. Read communication arm—so that the thrusts of the pastor and teachers, the programs and projects of the church can benefit from each and every means of communication available today. Plays can certainly provide original material encompassing questions, challenges, and carefully presented guideposts as the church desires, but also can serve effectively in augmenting sermons and the teachings of pastor and leaders on any occasion as needed.

This book of plays offers material that may be used for just such purposes, and in the hands of devoted and hard-working people will serve the individual churches well. The plays herein have been chosen with a view of covering a wide variety of targets and will do so. They have all been proved by use across the United States, Canada, and (for that matter) the world by the professional ministry of the Covenant Players. Also each play is capable of hitting more than one target so that the plays will provide thought-challenges beyond the more obvious themes each presents.

In addition, use of the plays and a determined development of the church's communication group (the drama section) will plant seeds of thought that will last long after the production, and will, eventually, create a harvest of interest, learning, and commitment.

This medium *is* a powerful tool and should be utilized by every energetic and aware church so that no stone will be left unturned in the determination to promulgate the reality of the Christian message and solidify the convictions and commitments of the followers of Jesus Christ.

I pray and trust that this book, these plays, will prove to be of valuable assistance to one and all—that each user church and group will benefit from concerted use.

With God's greatest blessings.

Charles M. Tanner
Saratoga Hills, California

SOME BASIC INSTRUCTIONS

The art of drama is about *doing*—it is action, it is life. This is one reason it is such an effective form of communication for the gospel. It is, in fact, the most communicative of the art forms.

To develop viable ministry through drama, one must *do it*; there is no alternative approach. Live drama is just that—*live* drama. To present a play, one must first have the play itself, created and crafted by a writer. Then one must have a director to interpret the play, and then the performers to embody it. Each must do his or her part.

The plays in this volume have been proved effective by the doing of them. They are designed to be done with minimal sets and props in church chancels, halls, classrooms, or any open space. Done well and done prayerfully, they will communicate.

It is not the intent of these opening notes to provide a textbook for the director or the performer. These are simply some basics to help you get off on the right foot, to augment what may be available to you, or to inspire you to seek further information. Nothing replaces commitment, training, practice, and hard work. If you have questions concerning any of the material in this volume, or are seeking further resources, please write to Convenant Players, P.O. Box 2900, Oxnard, CA 93034-2900.

GETTING STARTED

To begin you will need some basic ingredients: the play, the performers, the director, the projected audience, the performance space, the necessary rehearsal time, deadlines, and (as in all faithful ministry) you should have commitment to the project.

PREPARATION

The Director: The job of the director is to interpret the play—to see that the truth and communication value written into the play actually arrives in the hearts and minds of members of the audience. Simply put, he or she poses as the audience, seeing to it that the play is, in fact, communicating to that audience. With rare exceptions, the performers cannot do this because they are too subjectively involved in the play itself, which is as it should be.

The director designs the set, plans the movement (blocking), brings the necessary production elements together (props, set pieces, etc.), and runs rehearsals, seeing to it that the performers are relating to one another in character, consistent with the truth of the play—real people really relating.

The Performer: The performer embodies the character. Learning the lines and the blocking is just step one. One then seeks to understand not only what is said, but why the character one is playing says it, to whom, and what exactly is really meant. One can say the phrase *Good Morning*, and mean all manner of things by it. The performer's goal is to "become" the person (character) the writer created, to *know* what each line said really means, and to talk to and listen to the other people (characters) in the world of the play. Again, real people really relating.

Always remember that the performers should seek to mold themselves to the character, not the other way around. The director should facilitate the process. Performing, directing, and writing are three totally different disciplines. Performers (especially those newer to the craft) have a tendency to forget this. This is most readily exemplified by people who change the lines in a play because they "feel" better another way, or (often more truthfully) because the performer doesn't understand them the way they are written. The simple answer is to work to understand the truth of the play. A play is crafted by the writer with rhythm and meter to the lines, and characterization is incorporated in the word choices. Every part and piece is there for a reason. Change or remove any part, and you detract from the whole, possibly disastrously. Nor should the performers direct, because they lack perspective, seeing the play as they do from the single subjective point of the characters they are portraying. Equally, the director should look at the play as a whole, as an entity, and not try to direct each part as if they were playing it themselves.

The Writer: Let the writer create; it is enough for the director to interpret and the performer to embody. The writer can't do the task of either of the others—each needs the others (refer to chapter 12 of Paul's Letter to the Church in Rome).

REHEARSALS

How much rehearsal time do you need? As much as it takes to get the play ready for a solid, polished performance. The play needs to be directed, the performers need to *own* their roles, and the production must be prepared. This is where deadlines become important. Generally speaking, for the plays in this volume, an intense time of concentration is the best way—say three or four rehearsals within the week or so leading up to the performance.

Here is a suggested format. The amount of time spent in each step will depend on the length and complexity of the play, and the capacity and experience of the director and performers:

1. *The Reading.* Gather the performers together for a "reading" of the play. Read the play together and have the director share both the vision for the production and some thoughts about what story the play tells, the world (environment, atmosphere) of the play, and how the characters are to be played. You want each performer to have a general sense of who they are in the play so that they can memorize their lines *before* the next rehearsal. Set a rehearsal schedule, make expectations clear, and establish deadlines.

2. *First Rehearsal.* Performers should come with their lines learned, and the director should come prepared with the set design and blocking (movement) for the play. The play is blocked—with the performers writing the movement, gestures, and so on down on their scripts so they have it to study and prepare for the next rehearsal. Have the performers actually move through it so that their bodies become accustomed to matching words with movement. You should allow enough time to get through the play at least twice.

3. *Polish Rehearsal.* Performers should be "off book" (know their lines and blocking). You may want to take the play in sections, a page or two at a time, and keep going over it until the lines and blocking flow smoothly. It is critical to get these mechanical things out of the way so that you can begin to concentrate on the relationships between the characters and the world of the play. Your goal is to have people really talking to and listening to one another and moving with motivation (purpose).

4. *Flow Rehearsal.* Sometimes referred to as "Dress Rehearsal." You should flow the play from beginning to end exactly as you intend to do it in performance—with props, costumes, full vocal projection, etc. Plan to get through the play at least twice, if at all possible, with a break for "notes" from the director between the run-throughs.

Note please that each participant should do his or her particular job between rehearsals. The director and performers should come prepared to strive toward the goals of each rehearsal. If not, then you will need to spend rehearsal time doing what should have been done on their own. This will obviously increase the amount of rehearsal time you need.

Also, here are some suggested "Rules" for rehearsal etiquette which, if clearly understood by all, should make rehearsal an enjoyable and productive endeavor:

1. Be on time and come prepared to work.
2. Treat everyone with mutual New Testament respect.
3. The director is always right (performers don't argue).
4. When the director is wrong, refer to Rule #3.
5. Directors are courteous to the performers.
6. Concentrate on the task at hand.
7. Do not take yourself seriously—take what you are doing *very* seriously.

STAGING THE PLAY

Use the *K.I.S.S.* approach—*Keep It Straightforward and Simple*. The plays you have here are specifically crafted for this kind of approach. Use only what you need. This will direct the focus of the audience to the play itself.

From the introductory material provided for each play, and by careful reading, you will be able to determine what are the necessary set and prop requirements for production. It is recommended that you set up each play by describing the scene to your audience. This allows for the minimal use of set pieces and props and involves your audience through the use of their imagination. In some cases, the scene description will include optional set pieces or props. Use them if it is helpful to your production; otherwise, let them be fuel for the imaginations of your audience.

First, examine the requirements of the play. Define your minimum set and prop needs. Set pieces (chairs, tables, etc.), entrances and exits, hand props, and so on. It really helps to make lists.

Second, examine your stage area. What kind of space do you have? What are the sight lines of your audience? Are there lighting or sound limitations? Remember, your performers must be seen and heard.

Third, how much space is needed for the movement? Remember, a play should have motivated movement to be dynamic.

Now, your goal is to arrange the minimal requirements on the space available in such a way as to allow for the necessary movement, keep the set balanced, provide dynamic angles, and give the audience the best possible view of the performers (their eyes and faces).

MOVEMENT (BLOCKING)

When providing movement for a play, remember these keys:

1. You need movement to keep the play dynamic.
2. You want to keep it balanced. (Don't have four characters all walk to the same side of the stage at the same time. Your stage will "sink").
3. Keep your performers open to the audience—eyes and faces visible—not only when they are speaking, but when they are reacting to others.
4. Provide each performer with a realistic hand prop—something to work with in their hands.
5. Motivate the movement. People do things for *reasons*. The characters in the play must move for reasons. The motivations can be mechanical (to get a cup of coffee), emotional (to hide their fear), psychological (they are lying), or intellectual (they are distracting someone).

TECHNICAL SUPPORT

It is best to stick to the basic rule that the performers must be heard and seen. If you have a facility that provides for good light control and you have the chance to rehearse with it, well and good. If you have a good sound system that will allow the performers to move freely and amplify them evenly and you can rehearse with it, go for it. But you do not necessarily need these things. Remember *K.I.S.S.: K*eep *I*t *S*traightforward and *S*imple—the performers must be seen and heard.

RESOURCES

If you have access to professionals who share your commitment and communication goals, use them. What has God provided you in your fellowship? Put God's gifts to use. If you desire more detailed information, write to us and we'll help or put you in touch with someone who can. We all share the goal of challenging and life-changing communication of the gospel of Jesus Christ.

A WORD ABOUT ATTITUDE

Positive commitment to thorough and concentrated work is first and foremost the necessary attitude. The Lord asks for our first fruits—our very best. If drama is to be done as ministry, it should be done with an attitude of ministry—of positive commitment. In this case, that means that all involved share a first priority: the play itself—the communication value and power that it contains. The goal is not to "wow" an audience, to impress them with stagecraft or acting ability, or to merely entertain them as an end in and of itself. Real depth communication demands that the audience become involved in the world of the play (empathy). Every participant should keep this firmly in mind. More than ever, as Shakespeare said, the *play* is the thing.

The overall success of the play becomes the shared vision, which transcends individual egos and personal agendas. Each seeks to support and enable the other. The performance becomes an act of love, expressing a commitment to God, the play, the audience, and those involved.

Ultimately, it must be remembered that the Holy Spirit is available to work through the material so that it may impact and change lives. Cover your work in prayer.

Now, do it and enjoy!

THE SCRIPT ITSELF

When you begin working with the script itself, you will find that the writer has provided a wealth of good information for both the director and the actor in the parenthetical notes. These may relate to action that is to happen, mechanical delivery of the line, atmospheric considerations for the director to interpret, character information for the actor to embody, or any combination of these things.

The dialogue (or the "line") is "broken up" in a variety of ways. The term "beat" and its variations indicates a break or brief pause in the line and illuminates the character's thoughts. Punctuation is also used to break up the lines, so that they play as real conversation. For example, a dash at the end of a line indicates a cut-off or abrupt stop, whereas an ellipses (. . .) indicates a trailing off of the line or thought.

Always remember that the dialogue is written to be *spoken*—carefully crafted with word choice, punctuation, and parenthetical notes to dramaturgically embody actual speech. It does not necessarily reflect written grammatical correctness–people don't speak that way. As you work with the material you will find the dialogue has rhythm and meter written into the structure of the lines themselves.

PROP LIST

ONE IN ONE SIXTY-EIGHT
1. Water hose
2. Bible

SHORT CHANGE
1. Purse
2. Checkbook
3. Wallet
4. Dollar bill
5. Offering plate
6. Church bulletins
7. Hymnal
8. Pew bench (or 2-3 chairs)

GOOD SENSE—THAT'S WHAT IT IS
1. 2 coffee cups

ONE SUNDAY MORNING
1. Purse
2. Bible or 2
3. Church bulletins

CHOSEN ON PURPOSE
1. Children's large ball
2. Children's ball and bat
3. Doll
4. Stools
5. Small table
6. Plastic lids from small containers (apple sauce, cottage cheese, sour cream, margarine)
7. Wide-tip felt markers
8. Tray
9. Cookies
10. Apron

LIVING WATER
1. Patio (or card) table
2. Chairs for table
3. Tall plants (if possible or smaller plants on stands)
4. Ceramic pitcher and cup (if possible)

TO CARE IS THE QUESTION
1. Table
2. Chairs
3. Coffee cups/water glasses
4. Cream pitcher/sugar bowl
5. Napkins/knife/fork/spoon (2 each)
6. Plate and sweet roll (2 each)

A REQUEST FOR A COAT
1. Sofa (or 3 chairs)
2. Easy chair (or folding/stacking chair)
3. Coffee table (with magazines)
4. Small bookshelf with books and knick knacks
5. Small table
6. T-square/pens/drafting paper/wood modeling tools/pencils/calculator
7. Plates/forks/spoons/tray/napkins
8. Sugar/cream
9. Cake

THE TIE THAT BINDS
1. Table
2. Chairs
3. Coffee pot
4. Coffee cups/cream/sugar/spoons
5. Newspaper

IF YOU DON'T LIKE THE FACTS, CHANGE THEM
1. 3 tables
2. 6 chairs
3. Plates/sweet rolls/glasses/cream/sugar/napkins/knives/forks/spoons
4. Coffee pot/coffee cups/water pitcher
5. Restaurant order tickets

ONE IN ONE SIXTY-EIGHT

Charles M. Tanner

Scene: Either role can be played for either gender. Just use the right kind of name and adjust the personal pronouns to the performer. This is backyard talk—across a hedge, a fence, or just on two adjoining yards. The first person on stage is dressed for church, the next comes on—from the opposite stage entrance, of course, in very casual attire. As the latter comes on, he/she stops, shakes head, and smiles ruefully; then approaches the other zestfully.

Geo: *(For George or Georgette)* Hi good neighbor. *(Big smile as the other turns, water hose in hand)* You don't look dressed for church.

Kim: *(Turns, either way, is not happy to see the other but forces a darn-it smile and shake of the head)* Yeah. You're right. *(Beat, flat)* Son of a gun.

Geo: *(Looking at watch)* Well, fortunately you've plenty of time. *(Half beat, smile)* I'll wait for you.

Kim: *(Still flat and disapproving)* I went to church LAST week.

Geo: *(Laughs)* The Lord is still the Lord, Kim. All this week, too. *(Grins to take the sting out)*

Kim: *(Grimace)* Funny. *(Looks at lawn)* I've got to water my lawn.

Geo: *(Solemnly)* Kim, I promise you. Personally. Your lawn won't go anywhere. It'll be here after church.

Kim: *(Makes a face)* I had other things planned for this afternoon. Important things.

Geo: *(Surprised)* More important than the Lord?

Kim: I can worship the Lord here.

Geo: *(Laughs lightly—taking sting out)* How, Kim?

Kim: *(Startled, stares at the other)* Meditation. You know.

Geo: *(Smiling)* Afraid not. Tell you what—you come to church with me this morning, and then when we return—oh, that important business of yours—well, sometime next week, you'll teach me how to worship the Lord through meditation, and *(big smile)* I'll join you in that NEXT week.

Kim: *(Stares)* You're stubborn. You know that?

Geo: *(Nods)* About some things. Some PRIORITY things, yes, I guess so. We were told to be. *(Grins)* New Testament.

Kim: *(Sighs)* Look, the Lord knows who I am.

Geo: *(Gently)* "I am." *(Beat)* Interesting you should say just that. I think it's vitally important we acknowledge who the *first* I AM is—*(A warm smile)* Don't you?

Kim: *(Stares)* Oh, man!

Geo: *(Small laugh)* Good. Got that straight. *(A smile)* Look, Kim, the Lord supports you every moment. Lifts you up. Sustains you. Is ever ready to come to your aid. Answers your prayers. Maintains life. *(A plea)* Isn't that so?

Kim: *(Big vague gesture)* Well, yeah—but . . .

Geo: *(Nods)* Standing up for Him, being present among His people—His faithful followers—worshiping Him who is the First I AM, the Living God of the ages . . . Isn't that—the first priority?

Kim: *(Less irritated)* Every week?

Geo: *(Nods, grinning)* Right. Every week. One hour. One hour in one hundred sixty-eight hours the Lord gives you each week.

Kim: *(Tosses down the hose, slight nod, then a shrug)* Okay. You got through to me. I'll go change. *(Starts off, at the door, turns back and sighing, but with a small smile)* Let us go up to the House of the Lord. *(Another shrug and exits)*

Geo: *(Nods, a gentle, loving smile)* And with gladness, good neighbor, good friend, brother. *(Nods emphatically)* I was glad when they said unto me. . . .

(He/she freezes and the lights dim out or the curtain closes.)

THE END

SHORT CHANGE

Charles M. Tanner

Scene: Church—Sunday morning, two chairs side by side. Two friends—the glazed look or the mesmerized look as the anthem is just finished.

Terry: Boy! That piece always gets to me. That Jesu, etc. Joy of Man's whatever. Beautiful, just beautiful.

Pat: Yes, it certainly is. Bach was a fantastic genius. No question about it.

Terry: No question. He sure was. Beautiful.

Pat: Did you know? I read once where Bach got only a total of $23.00 for that music. Think of it! Only $23.00.

Terry: Well, that's not so bad. After all—that ability to write that music—God gave it to him, didn't He? *(A beat)* God gave him what he got—he should share it!

(Usher comes and Pat puts in an envelope—his pledge. Terry drops in some change—or a one dollar bill. Pat stares at him as the usher leaves.)

Pat: You just put in a one dollar bill. *(A beat)* Hmmm. You poor guy. What a shame!

Terry: What do you mean?

Pat: Considering what you're sharing—wow! You sure got short-changed, didn't you? *(Freeze, beat, and curtain)*

THE END

GOOD SENSE—THAT'S WHAT IT IS

Charles M. Tanner

Scene:	Two friends walking together in a park or similar friendly chit-chat setting. Either gender mix is possible—adjust the personal pronouns as necessary.

Phil: Do you believe in prayer?

Toni: Heavens no!

Phil: Why not?

Toni: Waste of time. God and I aren't on the same wave length.

Phil: Excuse me, I thought you were a Christian.

Toni: Well, I am. Of course.

Phil: I don't follow you. God and you aren't on the same wave length—yet you are a Christian?

Toni: Look, God is infinite right? I'm finite. He loves me, I—uh—love him. You know. I don't have to talk to Him. He knows where I stand.

Phil: That's very interesting.

Toni: Good sense. That's what it is. *(A beat)* Why'd you bring that up anyway?

Phil: I thought it might help you with—a problem. *(A beat)* You look very troubled.

Toni: I am. Deep trouble. Very bad.

Phil: I'm sorry. *(Half beat)* Could, uh, I help?

Toni: No. Thanks anyway. Nothing you could do.

Phil: *(Slowly)* I see.

Toni: It's Mary. I'm afraid she *(beat)* doesn't love me anymore.

Phil: I don't believe that. I'm sure she loves you. *(Looks down, reflects, then looks at Toni)* Why do YOU think she doesn't love you anymore?

Toni: She doesn't tell me she loves me. *(Shrugs)* She doesn't talk to me.

THE END

ONE SUNDAY MORNING

Charles M. Tanner

Scene: It is a beautiful Sunday morning—or it is raining, snowing, or sleeting—and a young (or old) couple are on their way home following the worship service. A standard normal conversation in such circumstances.

Jean: That was a GOOD sermon, today.

Bob: Yeah, for a change.

Jean: Bob!

Bob: I call 'em as I see 'em.

Jean: It's not very Christian.

Bob: It's Christian to tell the truth.

Jean: Yes, but always?

Bob: Whaddya mean by that?

Jean: Just what I said.

Bob: Thanks a lot.

Jean: Don't be pious about it.

Bob: Pious!

Jean: You don't like piety—remember?

Bob: Okay, okay, but he's sure long winded some of the time.

Jean: Involvement is a good subject.

Bob: Yeah, I could spot a dozen guys I hope were listening.

Jean: I certainly spotted one.

Bob: You're fast with the needles today.

Jean: Sorry, dear. I meant, me, too!

Bob: You're right, of course.

Jean: Oh Bob!

Bob: What?

Jean: Look! Over there. That man. He looks hurt—or sick.

Bob: He looks drunk to me.

Jean: This time of day? On Sunday?

Bob: Doesn't make any difference to a lush. C'mon.

Jean: We ought to help him.

Bob: You can't help a drunk. Let's go. It's late. We'll miss the whole game.

Jean: I think he's sick.

Bob: I think he's drunk. Let's go home.

Jean: Surely the TV can wait. Bob he's—

Bob: *(Cuts in)* Bombed out of his mind *(Starts to move off)*.

Jean: Bob, wait, he's falling. I think he's gasping for air. *(Desperately)* He is sick.

Bob: It's getting late, come on!

Jean: He needs help!

Bob: Jean, will you come on. There's lots of people to help.

Jean: I feel I should do something.

Bob: You can't do everything. Let someone else do it.

Jean: But, Bob.

Bob: Let someone else do it, Jean, for heaven's sake!

Jean: If he's having a heart attack, he'll die.

Bob: Jean, it isn't your problem. Now come on. Today's game is *important*.

Jean: *(Starts off hesitantly)* I feel so awful, we should—

Bob: *(Cuts in)* Stay out of it. Getting into something like that could mean real trouble. Real trouble. We could get really involved.

(Silence)

THE END

CHOSEN ON PURPOSE

Charles M. Tanner

CAST

Kenny Koala ....A boy Koala
Kathy Koala ....A girl Koala who is a neighbor
Mum Koala ....Kenny's Mother

Notes: This calls for some creative staging. If desired, costuming can be achieved with simply made head-pieces and gloves, and the use of dark colored turtlenecks and the like. Children have wonderful imaginations, so you can certainly put that to use for whatever you lack. All the rules of drama apply to children's material—play it straight, they'll get it (probably ahead of the adults).

Scene: A eucalyptus tree—a big one—and a special one because this is the home of Kenny and Kerry Koala (brother and sister, respectively) and Mama and Papa Koala. Their house is in the tree. Lightning made a marvelous cave inside the huge trunk of the tree but left enough that it still remained alive and even continued to grow. There is a nice playing yard out front and scattered around can be seen some Koala toys—balls, mostly, and some wood that's made kind of like a cricket bat. This is Australia, after all. There is something that serves as a table and two stools. At CURTAIN, Kenny is working on some things at the table—tops from plastic tubs (margarine, sour cream, cottage cheese, etc.). He should have a half-dozen of these. He is printing with a large, used marker. In the background we see another young Koala girl, Kathy—a neighbor—standing at the edge of the stage, looking downcast and wistful.

Kenny: *(Whistling or humming tunelessly while he works. After a while he looks up and sees Kathy Koala standing there. But she's a girl, so he shrugs and goes back to work)* Kerry's not here.

Kathy: *(Another small blow in life. She doesn't move)* Oh.

Kenny: *(Works awhile, looks up again)* I don't know when she'll be back.

Kathy: *(Nods glumly)* Uh huh. *(Longish beat)* Uh, what're you doing, Kenny?

Kenny: *(Perks up at that, holds up a plastic cover)* I'm making badges.

Kathy: *(Doesn't understand)* Badges?

Kenny: *(Goes back to work, tongue out, working intensely)* Yep. Badges. *(Beat)* Good ones, too.

Kathy: *(One step in, trying to see, but too shy to come further)* What are badges?

Kenny: *(A look at her. Dumb girl!!)* Badges are what you wear. What you wear when you're special—and like that.

Kathy: *(Interested)* Oh? *(Beat)* That sounds—wonderful. *(Innocently)* Who're they for?

Kenny: *(Proudly, taps his chest)* Me. *(Shrugs)* And a few others, of course.

Kathy: *(Almost a smile)* That sounds very nice. *(On her tip-toes trying to see)* They look like very nice things.

Kenny: *(Growls)* Not things—not just things, for goodness' sake. Badges. Badges are very special. *(Beat)* Only special people get to wear them.

Kathy: *(Nods)* I suppose that's right. Very special thin—uh—badges. *(Beat)* People who get one of those must be very lucky.

Kenny: *(A smaller growl)* We don't believe in luck in my family. We believe in the Lord, and He takes care of us. *(Proudly)* We don't have to have luck. He takes care of us.

Kathy: *(Sighs)* That must be very nice.

Kenny: *(Fast and hearty)* You bet it is! Great! *(Beat, while working)* If you hadda have only luck you wouldn't have very much, my Dad says. *(Looks at her, the young preacher-teacher)* 'Cause then your luck could be bad as well as good. There wouldn't be any reason for it. Just good luck once in a while and then a lotta bad luck most of the time.

Kathy: *(Sighs again)* I think my Momma and Daddy only believe in luck. *(Looks down sadly)* We mostly have bad luck. *(Looks off and twists a toe in the ground)* At least I do. *(Beat)* But then I suppose my Momma does, too. Have bad luck—mostly. *(A tear appears)* My Daddy, too, must have lots of bad luck. None of us ever get much good luck.

Kenny: *(The world is simple to him, a bit sharply)* Well then, stop believin' in luck. That's all. Let the Lord take care of things for you.

Kathy: *(Nods firmly)* I'd like that.

Kenny: *(Sniffs)* Well then, just do it. *(Mutters)* Golly, girls are dumb sometimes.

Kathy: *(A bit of energy)* I don't think it's dumb when you don't know some things. I mean when no one tells you about them.

Kenny: *(The small bark)* Well, I just told you about this one. So—just do it.

Kathy: *(Shrugs)* I'm afraid I don't know how to—do that. *(A sigh)* It doesn't sound very easy to me.

Kenny: *(Straightens up—it is to him)* It is easy. Just DO it. *(Frowns)* I mean— what's so hard about it? Believe the Lord will help you and—*(can't think of what else)* and He will. That's all.

Kathy:	*(Wants to please him)* All right. *(Beat and a small shrug)* I'll TRY. *(Beat)* But I don't know how to believe that, I guess.
Kenny:	*(Snaps)* Just *do* it.
Kathy:	*(Afraid he'll send her away)* All right, Kenny. I WILL. *(She closes her eyes and grits her teeth and tightens her hands into fists.)* I'm trying.
Kenny:	*(Sees her actions, grimaces and shakes his head)* Yeah, I can see that.
Kathy:	*(After Kenny works awhile, she relaxes and looks hopefully at him)* Does something happen? How do I know if my believing works?
Kenny:	*(Turns to her and thinks, Wow, how dumb can you get? But he sees she needs help and something in him responds to that)* Well, just think of the thing you want most in the world—think hard—and ask the Lord to give it to you. *(Frowns)* That's all.
Kathy:	*(Eyes wide)* That's all?
Kenny:	*(Nods)* Yep. That's all. *(Beat)* But it may take some time, you know. The Lord has a lotta people asking Him for things and He has to answer all these that He gets asked. *(Assumes a condescending attitude)* It takes time to get all those things answered. *(But he does have some real wisdom)* You hafta be willing to wait 'til He answers those who asked first. *(Proud of his knowledge and values)* That's only fair, of course.
Kathy:	*(Big-eyed)* Oh, I'll be patient. I've never asked—the Lord—for anything before. *(Worried)* He may not know me. *(More worried)* Will He answer me if He doesn't know me?
Kenny:	*(Has to think about this one)* I don't know. *(Thinks hard)* I think He knows everybody. *(Big open sigh)* I don't know if He can do *that.* *(Importantly)* I know a lot of people but *I* don't know everybody. *(Amazed)* Not even everybody in this forest. *(Sure though)* But Mum and Dad SAY that He knows all the people in the world. *(Helpfully)* That's even more than this whole forest. *(Firm about this)* And if my Mum and Dad say it is so, then it must be so.
Kathy:	*(Impressed immensely with him and his family, hastily but in truth)* I believe you. If YOUR Mum and Dad say it is so, I am sure it is the truth.
Kenny:	*(Nods, but proud inside)* Of course it is.
Kathy:	*(Another sigh as she thinks about it)* Your Mum and Dad sound so very nice. You're luck—I mean you've been answered good, very good.
Kenny:	*(Nods)* Yep. I sure have. *(Then a stare at her)* Haven't your Mum and Dad told you about the Lord at all? About His answering you—an' like that?

Kathy: *(Slowly shakes her head)* No. *(Looks off)* My Mum and my Dad don't live together anymore. They're not lucky at all. That's what they say. I guess the Lord doesn't answer them.

Kenny: *(It's still simple)* That's because they don't ask Him for answers.

Kathy: *(Nods)* I know. *(Softly)* I never have either.

Kenny: *(Leans toward her, firmly)* Well, you have now. *(Beat)* Haven't you?

Kathy: *(Concerned he might think her dumb again)* I'm going to.

Kenny: *(Nods at her)* Well, go ahead. *(Understands that she needs to be alone in this, turns to his work)* You ask. I'll finish my work. *(She nods and bows her head and closes her eyes. Again we see how intensely she's concentrating. He works but occasionally he flicks a peek at her and then returns to his work. Finally she opens her eyes)*

Kathy: *(Wide-eyed, a new experience for her)* There, I did it. I asked Him.

Kenny: *(A challenging look)* For the thing you want most?

Kathy: *(Nods slowly)* Yes. The thing I want more than anything else in the world.

Kenny: *(Shrugs)* You don't have to tell anybody what you asked for, but I suppose you could tell your Mum. *(Beat, then it hits him. Amazed)* Your Mum and Dad don't live together? *(Can't understand that)* How come? *(Beat)* I mean that's what parents are for—to live in your house and be there for you. *(Beat)* I don't get it.

Kathy: *(Shrugs)* They are what is called divorced. *(Frowns)* That means they don't— *(tears)* don't like each other any more. And don't want to live together *(beat)* ever again. *(Turns and cries. He's shocked and out of his ken.)*

Kenny: *(Doesn't know what to do)* Hey? That's—awful. *(Thinks)* But how can they be parents if they live apart from you?

Kathy: *(Shrugs, her back to him)* I don't know. I live with my Mum. But she's not happy, and I kinda get in the way, I think.

Kenny: *(Deep, deep frown)* How can you get in the way? You're her little girl, aren't you?

Kathy: *(Nods)* Yes, but . . . well, grown-ups are kind of funny sometimes. *(Quickly)* My Mum is nice, but she has lots of things to worry about, I guess.

Kenny:	*(Concerned now)* You don't have any brothers or sisters, do you?
Kathy:	*(Shakes her head)* No. There's just me.
Kenny:	*(Looks away, bites his lip)* That's too bad. *(Shrugs)* I'm sorry, Kathy.
Kathy:	*(A wan smile)* You're very nice, Kenny. *(Beat)* Nobody has ever said they were sorry to me before. That's nice of you.
Kenny:	*(Careful, he says to himself)* Wellll . . . *(Shrugs)* My Mum and Dad care for me. They care for each other, too. *(Frowns)* It must be very hard not to have your Mum and Dad—care for you.
Kathy:	*(Quickly)* Oh, I'm sure they do. They're just so busy—and I never see them together. *(Looks off)* I see my Father sometimes, too. *(Shakes her head)* He's not very happy and seems worried an' everything, too.
Kenny:	*(Understands some of her behavior)* Golly, it must be very lonely. Being an only kid and not having your parents together.
Kathy:	*(Nods, feeling it but getting real help from his questions)* It's very lonely. *(Then suddenly)* I hate it! *(And she turns away from him and cries again)*
Kenny:	*(At a loss)* Uh—golly. Don't cry. *(Longish beat while he tries to think of something he could say or do)* Uh, want to see my badges?
Kathy:	*(An almost instant stop of tears as children can do, turns and wiping her eyes, tries to look happier)* Oh, yes, I would like that very much.
Kenny:	*(Brusquely to cover his unmanly feelings)* Well. You can't see anything over there. *(Glares)* And I'm not bringing them to you.
Kathy:	*(Quickly)* Oh. Of course. *(And she hurries over to him)*
Kenny:	*(Holding one for her—an unfinished top)* See these are tops I found. Aren't they great?
Kathy:	*(Stares at the clear plastic circle. Anything he thinks is great at this stage she thinks is great. If he claimed a blade of grass great, she'd agree wholeheartedly)* Oh, yes. Those things are—great. *(A beat)* Is that the badge?
Kenny:	*(Sniffs)* No, no, these are just the tops. I found these. *(Holds up a marker)* I found this, too. *(Shrugs)* There were others but they were all worn out. *(Proudly)* But this one has some good ink in it still. *(He proves it by making a mark on paper)*

Kathy: *(Eyes aglow)* It makes a very big mark, doesn't it?

Kenny: *(The expert)* That's what you have to have when you're making badges. *(Super expert)* Regular pens won't make a mark on these things.

Kathy: *(Thinking he's clever)* That's very smart of you to know that.

Kenny: *(He's also ingenuous)* I found that out when I tried pens. They didn't work. Then I found these things. *(Laughs)* Humans throw away a lot of good things. *(Leans toward her a bit)* Humans are crazy, you know. They do a lot of dumb things.

Kathy: *(Not very experienced with humans)* They do?

Kenny: *(The expert again)* Yeah. Like when they come and stare at us and try to get us to come down out of the tree and do something. *(The superior koala)* Do things? Like what?

Kathy: *(Shrugs, wide-eyed)* I don't know.

Kenny: *(Nods)* I don't either. Nobody knows. 'Specially the humans, I think. *(Looks at his treasures)* But they sure throw away a lotta good things.

Kathy: *(Eyeing the things)* They certainly do. *(Looks around)* But where are the badges?

Kenny: *(Stares at her)* I make them. Mum and Dad say I'm pretty smart to do the things I do. *(Naïveté)* I guess I am.

Kathy: *(Nods, admiringly)* I think you are.

Kenny: *(Goes back to the work)* I make them all myself. It's my idea, you know. *(Another shrug)* My Dad helped a little. But they're mostly my ideas. *(Holds one up)* See I put the word BADGE on first. *(To her)* That's so everyone will know what it is. *(She nods)* And then I fill the rest in. *(Reads it)* THE KOALA FAMILY CLUB. *(Then a big grin and pride, he shows it to her. She is very impressed)* See? That's us. *(The pride again)* Mum 'n' Dad 'n' Kerry 'n' me. We all belong to this club. That's special, you see.

Kathy: *(The tears again and in a low voice)* That's wonderful, Kenny. Very, very wonderful. You ARE lucky.

Kenny: *(Frowns)* Dad says we're not lucky, we're blessed.

Kathy: *(Softly)* VERY blessed. *(Turns away again)* I wish I belonged to something. Really, to someone.

Mum K: *(Kenny's Mum comes out with some special cookies)* I see you have a guest, Kenny, so I brought you out some special tender new eucalyptus leaf cookies. *(Smiles)* And some milk. *(To her)* Kerry's not here, Kathy, but I am glad you and Kenny are getting along so well.

Kathy: *(Nods, tries a smile, Mum sees the tear stains, immediately is filled with compassion)* Thank you, Mrs. Koala-Kerns.

Kenny: *(Suddenly)* Mum, Kathy doesn't have anything to belong to. That's awful. She's lonely. Can't we make her a part of our Family Club? Can't she be our sister?

Mum K: *(Is constantly being surprised by childish wisdom, tries to catch up, gently)* Well, Kenny, that would be nice, but Kathy has her own family.

Kenny: *(Blurts it out)* But her folks are divorced or something, and they don't live together with her. She stays with her Mum, but sometimes with her Dad, and they don't seem to know she's there.

Mum K: *(Covering)* Well, I'm sure they care for Kathy very much. *(To her)* It is a sad thing that your parents are separated. I know it must be difficult for you.

Kenny: *(Fast)* She hasn't got any brothers or sisters either. *(Eagerly)* She could be our sister. We only got one, and we could find room to care for another. Mum, can't we?

Mum K: *(Caught and hides her tears)* Yes, I guess we could call her—our sister. The Lord told us that was right. *(To her)* But won't your Mum—not like such an idea?

Kathy: *(Eagerly)* Oh no. *(Beat)* She's away from our house a lot. She wouldn't mind at all.

Kenny: *(Nods, big grin)* It's all right then, Mum?

Mum K: *(Sighs)* It will be all right to call her a sister, but she would have to stay living with her Mother.

Kathy: *(Fast and happily)* That'd be all right, Mrs. Koala-Kerns. I'd like that very much. *(She smiles, too)*

Kenny: *(Big grin)* Great! *(They smile at each other)*

Mum K: *(Looks off thoughtfully)* I'd better go and talk with your Mother, Kathy. We want to be sure we don't make her unhappy. *(Smiles)* Grown-ups need care, too, you know.

Kenny: *(Thinks)* I guess so.

Kathy: *(Concerned)* She may not be home, but I'm sure it'll be all right.

Mum K: *(Smiles at her)* Enjoy the cookies, dear. You ARE a very nice little girl. AND you are—important! *(And with that she exits on her way to Kathy's Mum)*

Kenny: *(Proudly)* My Mum's great, isn't she?

Kathy: *(A beaming smile)* I think you're great, too, Kenny.

Kenny: *(Embarrassed, turns to the table)* Well, now that you're a sister, I'd better make you a badge, too.

Kathy: *(Happily, suddenly leans over and kisses him on the cheek. He leaps back in horror.)* You're a very nice brother.

Kenny: *(Growls)* Hey, just remember somethin'. I don't allow sisters to kiss me. *(Growls again)* It's embarrassing.

Kathy: *(Easily)* Not to me. *(Nods)* I guess I will have a lot to learn. *(Beat, gently)* How to-belong-to something-some body. (Looks around, eyes glistening) A brother, a sister, and a Family CLUB. *(Suddenly her eyes open wide and she covers her mouth)* OH!

Kenny: *(Stares at her)* What's the matter?

Kathy: *(Looks at him in awe)* I got answered. And so fast!

Kenny: *(Stares)* What d'you mean?

Kathy: *(Eyes wet and a smile, too)* I got what I asked for. The very first time. I asked the Lord for someone—something—to belong to. *(Awed)* And He gave it to me—right away! *(A longish beat while she thinks of it)* And now I'm a member of the Koala Family Club! *(He nods and grins proudly and hands her a badge, and she stares at it and is blissfully happy, with a look up at him. Seeing her look, he backs off fast before she can kiss him again. She laughs, and he shrugs and then grins and starts in on a cookie. Then she does, too. They are very happy)*

THE END

LIVING WATER

Charles M. Tanner

Scene: It could be an outer patio under a large fig tree, or an inner patio
surrounded by the walls of the house on two sides and a garden wall on
the third side; on the fourth side would be audience. At CURTAIN, a
woman is sitting beside a table, leaning forward and looking intently at her audience,
just slightly higher than that which the actress faces. She is intense, still excited and
happy to be speaking as she is at this moment.

Notes: This is a Singlet, a one-act *play* for one person. You must keep in mind
as you do it that it is not a monologue—it is a play, with conflict,
intellectual flow, rising and falling action—all the ingredients of a play.
The audience is part of the play, as inhabitants of her village who have come to hear
her story. The actress should perform as if she is speaking to the "villagers," but
without making direct eye contact with the actual audience members so as to preserve
the illusion. This can be done by the actress focusing her eyes just above the heads of
the live audience. The Scripture reference is John 4:1-42.

Romaliyah: I have come these many miles across our land to tell you, my family and
friends, of a wonderful thing that has happened to me. My family knows
who I am, for I was brought up in this house. But some of you here are
strangers to me. I have been away a long time. I am Romaliyah, and my
father was Jedizer—he who has been dead these past fifteen years. I
have just come from Sychar, near what Samaritans believe—even as did
I—is the Holy Mountain Mount Gerizim. But I have strange and happy
news for you. As you know, the Jews claim Jerusalem is the central place
to worship God, while our fathers tell us it is Mount Gerizim. I have odd,
but exciting news for you. It is neither. Or it will soon be neither for I
have been told so by the—Messiah himself. *(There is obviously a hubbub
at this point for she smiles and raises her hand.)* I know this is indeed
startling news. And you have the right to look questioningly at one
another. For truly I am what I am. As you can see and hear and as my
family knows, I am unlearned, and my life has been one of narrow,
twisting paths filled with rocks and thorns. I have not been a—clean
person, nor have I any importance whatsoever. Yet *(she dreams in a far-
off look for a moment)* the Messiah talked to me. He was a Jew. *(Again,
she raises her hand as the voices break out again)* I know. I know. We

Samaritans and Jews do not get along and I know that the Jews do look down upon us, but—*(a warm smile)* this man—did not. He asked me for water. *(Again a beat as though there is a murmur)* I was as surprised as you are and I asked him, "You, a Jew ask me for water? I am a Samaritan. How can you ask me for water?" *(Shrugs)* I did not mean to be rude, I was just so surprised by him speaking to me that I simply spoke as I thought. *(Frowns a little and squints her eyes in reflection)* Then he said a most surprising thing. "If you only knew what it is God can give, and who it is that is asking a drink of you, you would ask of him and he would give you your fill of Living Water." I stared at him. He was clearly weary from many miles of walking on the road, and he carried nothing with him. I later learned that his followers had gone on into the city to buy food while he rested by Jacob's Well. There was only this young man, John I think was his name, who was with him and just watched and listened. So I said to him, "Sir, you have no bucket and the well is deep. How could you possibly draw any water for me?" I thought that would stop him but I added "And where would you get living water? This is Jacob's Well, you don't claim to be greater than Jacob, do you?" *(She looks off again.)* He looked at me so searchingly, but somehow so warmly, and told me that whoever drank of this water would get thirsty again, but whoever drank of Living Water would never need to drink again because it would provide a spring in that person that would forever quench thirst and would give to that person eternal life. *(The buzz and then the halting raised hand)* Of course, I said, "Sir give me this water." *(She smiles and then slowly the smile fades)* But he bade me bring my husband. *(Shrugs sadly)* I—told him didn't have a husband. *(Almost gulps)* It was then that he told me all about myself and the things I had done, the way I had lived that no one knows but myself. *(Looks at them keenly)* For I have not been a—good person. But you see he told me things about me no one could possibly know. *(Shakes her head)* No way possible. *(Reflects a moment then shakes herself and continues)* I was stunned and all I could think to say when he had finished was, "I know that the Messiah called Christ will come, and when he comes he will tell us everything." *(She now looks away and gets that far-away look in her eye.)* He looked at me so piercingly that I would have looked away—if I could have. But I couldn't and then he said, very gently, "It is I. He who is talking to you." *(Exulting)* Oh, I knew it was true, and my spirit leaped within me—and then *(smiles)* so did I. I ran all the way into Sychar—and I am not a young girl—and found others and told them. And so strong was the spirit upon me that they believed everything I told them. *(A proud look)* Then they returned with me to the well and talked to the Messiah. The leaders of the city asked him to stay and tell them more. And he did—for two more days. *(Sighs pleasurably)* It was wonderful. *(Looks at them warmly)* And so I have come to tell you that you might believe. *(Her demeanor suggests that her information is being received positively. She nods her head and then looks off—far off into faraway inner space. Then as she speaks it is as to herself)* I don't think his own followers understood that he is the Messiah. That is strange. They are so learned and listen to him everyday. And I am so simple of mind. *(Shakes her head again)* I don't understand why *(A beat and then a radiant smile)* but I do understand him. *(Again a shake of her head even as the smile continues)* Isn't that a thing of wonder?

THE END

TO CARE IS THE QUESTION

Charles M. Tanner

CAST

Betty ....A bright young woman at a moment of truth.
Sue ....An equally intelligent—though currently forlorn—dry-witted young woman. She and Betty are roommates.

Scene: Could be a park bench, or could take place in a coffee shop at a table isolated a bit from others. Can be just the two people or with extras in the background. In any case, there are two people on stage when the scene opens. Sitting, enjoying each other's silent company.

Betty: *(After a quick look at the other, biting her lip, and then taking a deep breath)* I'm going home tomorrow—for the holidays.

Sue: Yeah, I know. *(Looking away)* Me, too. *(The latter without enthusiasm)*

Betty: I've debated talking to you about this. But I know I must.

Sue: *(Stares at her)* You mean I've got—bad breath?

Betty: *(No smile)* You know I'm a—Christian.

Sue: Yep. *(And for emphasis)* And I am not.

Betty: The Lord has so filled my life. I feel enriched and warm and cared for. It's a wonderful feeling.

Sue: *(A bit wistfully)* You're a happy kid.

Betty: *(Turns to her)* You don't seem happy—at any time, really.

Sue: It takes all kinds, and I don't have your accepting nature. That's all.

Betty: Wouldn't you want to be happy?

Sue: It's not in us Bakers. We're a gloomy group. You telling me you want a new roommate?

Betty: *(Laughs)* I should say not. I want—oh, I don't do this very well. There must be something wrong with me. But I would like with all my heart, more than anything in the world, for you—to—accept Christ.

Sue: *(Instant embarrassment)* Uh oh. I thought you were never going to buttonhole me.

Betty: *(Concerned)* Am I buttonholing you? I still don't want to do that. I won't pressure. And I'll not mention it again, unless you ask. But I do so want you to be happy. I do so want you to be a filled Christian.

Sue: Funny. The way you put it. That first you want me to be happy.

Betty: That's the reason I'm bringing this up. Badly, I'm afraid. I am not naturally a happy person, in spite of what you think. I am happy because I know—I must be careful about words—I really know, have this feeling inside me—that the Lord loves me.

Sue: I've heard that line before.

Betty: That's the trouble. Words can be used by anyone for any purpose and sometimes ill-used. I hope I'm not.

Sue: I know you're a sincere kid.

Betty: It's not a pat statement, Sue. That the Lord loves me. I, too, heard that all my life. Even took it for granted until I came to realize what it meant. That He—who made everything, all powerful and kind of gigantic—actually, warmly, uh—laughingly, happily, smilingly *loves* me. Cares for me, I—sometimes—feel as though His arm is about my shoulders. Not as it would be if He were in the midst of millions, but me, individually, on purpose and alone.

Sue: You—actually—believe that? I mean just as you've said it?

Betty: Yes. Actually. Just as I have said it and more. Oh, I wish I knew better speech patterns. I wish I could put it into exactly the right words to make you see.

Sue: *(Quietly)* You're doing pretty good.

Betty: *(Looks away)* I have strong feelings about the wrong kind of evangelism, but then it occurred to me, I don't know how to do the right kind, either.

Sue: But you feel you must? You mean it will help you if someone else believes what you—see?

Betty: *(Laughs quickly)* Oh no. That's just the opposite. I don't need anyone else to join me that I might feel I was doing the right thing. I never would buy a Chevrolet just because everybody else did. No, I don't need that. My strongest convictions come when I am alone.

Sue: Then why the agony? I mean it's clear to me you don't want to do this.

Betty: But I do want to. I just don't know how. I KNOW He has given me happiness. I want so very much for you to have this happiness, too.

Sue: You think it'll be the same for me?

Betty: No, I don't know about that. The same feelings, I mean. You would have your own way, but you would be filled and you would be enriched once you knew that He loves you just as much as anyone else.

Sue: *(Looking down)* Personally, you mean?

Betty: Yes, personally. You, Sue Baker, His beloved daughter.

Sue: *(Very low voice)* I don't like me.

Betty: *(Warmly)* I do. And I felt the same way about me until I came to realize that He who knew me better than anyone—knew all my faults and sins and miserableness—liked me anyway.

Sue: I wish I could believe that.

Betty: *(Smiles broadly)* Look at me and see an example of the facts of it. *(Sobered)* That, of course, is the final test of witness. If you cannot see it in me, then I have truly failed.

Sue: *(Still looking at her shoes, pauses, then in a wee, small voice)* You haven't failed.

Betty: *(Feeling tender)* Thank you for that, Sue. That helps.

Sue: *(After a beat)* Why did you wait so long to speak to me?

Betty: *(Staring at her)* Because I was afraid of buttonholing you.

Sue: *(Now looks at her under her eyebrows)* Then why did you talk to me today?

Betty: Going home did it, I guess. My wonderful warm family—all secure in the Lord. I looked at you and you looked so forlorn. *(Takes a deep breath)* You are my friend. I realized then that I cared for you so much, I could no longer be silent. *(A beat)* I cared for you enough to want you to know Christ, even if you disliked me for it. *(A beat)* That's it, I guess.

Sue: *(Looking down again)* You meant that invitation to spend the holidays with your family?

Betty: *(Brightens)* Of course, they all urged it emphatically. We'd love it.

Sue: All right. There's nothing at my home. I'll come. *(Shakes her head)* I know you mean it. *(Beat)* Then you can talk to me and help me to try to understand about—*(a small finger points up)*—Him.

Betty: *(Holds her face in her hands, her happiness bringing tears to her eyes)* Oh, Sue, I can't tell you. . . .

Sue: *(Sighs)* There must be something in it. *(Gets up and heads for the exit)* Classes. See you later. Yes, there must be something in it. *(Beat)* No one has ever cared that much for me before. *(Smiles, nods, and exits fast. Betty sits, filled with a sense of joy and wonder and reverent thanks for His participation in the miracle that just has happened. We have a slow CURTAIN to. . . .)*

THE END

A REQUEST FOR A COAT

Charles M. Tanner

CAST

Annie Dunn ....An educated accomplished woman who is married to Jimmy.

Jimmy Dunn ....An architect, designer, engineer who is an inventor. Struggling a bit right now.

Gates Burnside..........Now, a successful businessman. He is facing his past—and his present.

Scene: This is by intent a living room. But it can be a den, a patio, or even a family room—if any of these is more feasible. The usual sort of furniture—a sofa, a big chair or two, straight-backed chairs, table, small table, book shelves with not too many books, lamps, pictures, and decorative knick-knacks. On the table we see lots of papers, a slide rule, a triangle, perhaps a protractor, etc. The tools of a designer and builder are evident as well. We can even see, possibly, some parts and pieces of a model that Jimmy Dunn is building of what he has designed. As the scene opens we see him doing some drawing and then picks up the calculator, does some figuring and at the end, sits slumped in depression. He rubs his hands through his hair and conveys he's at his wit's end. The doorbell rings and he responds only to indicate that he heard it and then regains his slump. We hear a feminine voice and a masculine one answering; then, a moment later his wife, Annie, enters with another man—Gates Burnside.

Annie: *(To Jimmy, the polite manner suggesting the man is a stranger)* Jimmy, this is Mr. Gates Burnside. *(A half turn and a halfway apologetic look at the man)* I told him you were very busy but he insisted he must see you. Said it wouldn't take long.

Gates: *(Coming forward—a keen look in his eye)* It won't take long. *(Meaning it)* I AM sorry for insisting, but I'll only be in town a short time and—*(Ends lamely)* it's important.

Jimmy: *(Gets up, they shake hands)* That's all right. I'm stymied here anyway. *(To Annie, nicely with a sigh)* I need a break, my dear. *(Small smile)* How about some coffee?

Annie: *(Smiles back, knows how tired he is)* Certainly. I have some fresh cake, too.

Gates: *(Hurriedly)* Oh please, I don't want to bother you. I just have something to say and then I'll be on my way.

Annie: *(Soothing him)* It's all right, Mr. Burnside. Jimmy has been working night and day. Too hard. He's about burned out and can use a bit of a break. Please, be at ease. It will be good for him. *(She smiles again and leaves.)*

Jimmy: *(Standing and stretching)* Please, sit down, Mr. Burnside.

Gates: *(Starts to pace)* Thanks, but I need to pace about—if that doesn't bother you?

Jimmy: *(Shakes his head)* No, by all means. Enjoy our admiral's walk. *(Chuckles)* The carpet will have to suffice for that lofty area.

Gates: *(A searching look)* You don't know me, do you?

Jimmy: *(Looks him over and slowly shakes his head)* No. I'm afraid I don't.

Gates: *(Looks down)* There's no reason you should of course. *(Sighs)* But I know you.

Jimmy: *(A small smile)* Really? *(Short almost bitter laugh)* I didn't think I was that well known.

Gates: *(A straight look again)* You're an architect, aren't you?

Jimmy: *(Stretching again)* I used to be. I gave that up, perhaps mistakenly, a couple of years ago when I thought I had miraculously become a successful inventor.

Gates: *(A frown)* You mean you're not successful?

Jimmy: *(Ruefully)* I hope you're not from some agency checking my worth, Mr. Burnside.

Gates: *(Shakes his head)* No, no. Nothing like that at all.

Jimmy: *(Sighs)* Well then, I guess I can enjoy talking about my woes. *(Beat)* No. I am not a successful inventor. *(Hastily)* Oh, I've invented some things, and they seem to work all right. But I haven't had any success at it. Even the one thing that COULD do that for me, if I could get it off the ground.

Gates: *(Pressing, slight frown)* You mean an airplane, Mr. Dunn?

Jimmy: *(Laughs)* Nothing like that. *(Moves around the table, indicates the drawing and parts of a model—tubes, etc.)* It's a new kind of solar generator and retrieval system.

Gates: *(Is impressed)* Hmmmm. That seems to be on target for this time in history. Isn't that right?

Jimmy: *(Smiles)* Yes, indeed. The timing is right. *(Bitter again)* If I hurry. But there's a few bugs in my production opportunities.

Gates: *(Bites his lip)* May I ask what are those—bugs? A design problem?

Jimmy: *(Shakes his head)* No, the design is correct. *(Laughs shortly)* But you don't want to listen to my problems. *(A gesture of go ahead)* You wanted to see me?

Gates: *(Nods and then sighs again)* I'm afraid so. *(Jimmy stiffens a bit—bad news?)* I mean, the fear is mine. Not yours. *(Paces)* I hate saying this. I've covered it over for many years, but now it's got to come out, and it's one of the most painful things I've ever gone through.

Jimmy: *(Narrowed eyes)* You say it's not me—this so painful thing?

Gates: *(Hastily)* Yes, that's right. Not you. Me.

Annie: *(Brings in coffee, a carafe, cups and cakes, plates, and utensils)* Coffee and cake. *(Smiles)* I hope you like cake, Mr. Burnside?

Gates: *(Embarrassed)* Well, yes, I do. But I am sorry to put you out.

Annie: *(Smiles)* Now, Mr. Burnside, you've apologized enough. Let's hear no more of it. Just enjoy and we shall too.

Jimmy: *(Feeling he needs somebody here with him)* You have any objections to my wife being here, Mr. Burnside?

Gates: *(At first is horrified)* Good grief, yes, I do mind. *(But quickly)* But she should stay. I mean it bothers me because of what I have to say. But, of course, she has every right. And should stay. *(Rubs his forehead)* Please forgive me, both of you, but—*(Takes a deep breath)* The truth is . . . I am a thief.

Jimmy: *(They both stare at him)* You're a thief?

Annie: *(Looks at Jimmy)* I don't understand. *(Another look)* I mean, why come to our house and tell us that?

Jimmy: *(Nods)* What has it to do with us?

Gates: *(Sighs)* With you, Mr. Dunn. Not your wife. *(Shakes his head)* This is very difficult for me. *(To Jimmy, a plea in his eyes)* You see, fifteen years ago, I stole $400 from you. *(Rubs his face again)* A terrible and disgusting thing to do.

Jimmy: *(Stares at him)* You stole $400 from me. *(A deep frown)* Where was this?

Gates: *(The sad look)* At an architects' convention in Baltimore, Maryland.

Annie: *(To him fast)* You were at such a convention, Jimmy?

Jimmy: *(Knowledge begins to come)* That's right. And I did lose some money. *(Frowns deeper)* But that was an earlier time. I was having lots of problems—with myself. *(Makes his own face)* Drinking. I remember missing some money, but I didn't know how much I'd lost and what I'd tossed away. *(To Annie)* You knew of course I was drinking, but never mentioned the money. *(More frowns)* Did I?

Annie: *(At ease about it)* No. *(A weak smile)* At that time in our lives, I never knew what money you had and what you hadn't. *(A better smile)* That was a long time ago, Mr. Burnside. He hasn't had a drink in fourteen years.

Gates: *(A tilt of his head)* It was $400, all right. I took it out of your wallet. *(Beat)* That was a long time ago in my life, too. But I have just come around—very recently.

Jimmy: *(Not quite so friendly)* You look like you're doing all right.

Gates: *(Nods)* I am. I've made a bit of money. Have security—*(Bitter memories)* Whatever that means in today's world. And I've come into a legacy. Not very big, but substantial enough.

Annie: *(Gently)* And you've given up—things like—

Gates: *(A straight look at her)* Stealing? Oh, yes. But I did more than take your $400, Mr. Dunn. You had a check stub for the banquet proceedings. I stole that too. *(Jimmy shrugs)* The ticket won the main prize. *(Beat)* $1,000. *(Sighs)* So you see, I stole that, too.

Annie: *(A very low voice)* You kept that money?

Gates: *(Nods)* I'm afraid it didn't mean much to me then. But I promise you, it has given me hell ever since.

Annie: *(A small tilt of her head)* We'd like to have people stay out of hell, Mr. Burnside.

Gates: *(Nods)* Five months ago, I discovered the only way to stay out of that place. *(A better look)* I became a Christian.

Jimmy: *(Startled)* You did? *(To her)* That's amazing.

Annie: *(A good smile)* Yes, isn't it? *(To Gates)* We're very pleased. You see, Jimmy found the Lord shortly after that last drinking spree in Baltimore. *(Proudly)* He's been serving the Lord ever since.

Gates: *(Big beam too)* That's great. *(Shakes his head)* The Lord's ways are truly remarkable, aren't they? *(Looks off)* Most of my life I've been miserable, but too ignorant to know it. The last five months have been a mighty eye-opener for me.

Jimmy: *(Smiles)* Well, sit down and have some cake and coffee, now that you've got that off your chest. *(Firmly)* I know what it takes to speak up and clear a thing like that. *(A loving look at Annie)* I had to tell her something she may have guessed but didn't really know. *(To Gates encouragingly)* It's a bitter pill to have to swallow—to admit to your wife that you've been a drunk and a louse for years.

Annie: *(Gently)* We all make mistakes. *(Grins)* But I don't think this cake is. Please, Mr. Burnside.

Gates: *(Hesitantly)* I must first ask for your forgiveness. I am sorry. I have repented. If you'll forgive me, I can believe the Lord will.

Jimmy: *(With a wave)* You're forgiven. Totally. *(Chuckles)* Now that's done, and I am certain the Lord has forgiven you some time ago. Please, for goodness' sake, have some cake.

Gates: *(Happily)* One more thing. From what you say, this might come at the right time. *(Hands him a check)* I'm returning the money I stole from you.

Jimmy: *(Stares at him, looks at the check, whistles)* $3,000. *(Looks up, Annie reacts too)* This is a lot more than $400. *(Beat)* Even a lot more than $1400.

Gates: *(A small smile)* I added some punitive payments in there. *(Hand up)* For my conscience' sake. It is little enough. *(A real hope)* I hope that helps—your problem with your invention.

Jimmy: *(Grins)* It'll help a great deal. Keeping the wolf away from the door.

Annie: *(Smiling)* I should say so. *(Heartfelt)* Thank you, Mr. Burnside.

Gates: *(A smile)* I would feel a lot more forgiven if you could find your way to call me Gates. I'd like to be friends. *(Beat)* If that's possible.

Jimmy: *(Grabs his hand and shakes it)* Done—friend Gates. *(Chuckles)* I'm Jimmy.

Annie: *(To Gates)* In this family we give Christian brothers and sisters a hug. *(Hugs him, pulls back)* Welcome brother—and friend.

Gates: *(As he picks up the cake)* Will that help with the invention? *(Beat)* I take it your problem is money?

Jimmy: *(Modified happiness, shrugs)* It'll help keep the family going. *(Chuckles)* As you could guess—knowing the Lord, we're about out of all funds and nothing coming in. *(Looks down)* I'm about to give up and get a job as an architect again.

Gates: *(His face falls)* The $3,000 is not enough?

Jimmy: *(Shakes his head)* Afraid not.

Annie: *(Smiles)* If you don't start on the cake soon, Gates, a new friend is going to be in trouble.

Gates: *(Turns and smiles at her, takes the fork and starts to cut a bite, then looks up and sighs)* How much do you need?

Jimmy: *(Laughs shortly)* You really want to know?

Gates: *(Nods slowly)* Yes, I do. But just a minute. *(Takes out a notebook and a pen and writes briefly in it. Jimmy is puzzled and Annie interested. Gates lifts up his face and nods)* Tell me.

Jimmy: *(A lost expression and a big what-can-you-do gesture)* $75,000.

Gates: *(Nods)* The banks won't lend it?

Jimmy: *(Shakes his head)* I have no collateral.

Gates: The money is to build a prototype?

Jimmy: *(Nods again)* And set up the installation, get it going completely. *(Quickly)* The production model won't cost that much. In fact, that's what's so special about my invention. The price. The finished product won't cost even half as much as all current systems.

Gates: *(Puzzled)* Can't you get a loan against the obvious sales under such conditions?

Jimmy: *(Shakes his head)* No. The retailers—knowing that I have cracked the cost factor with my invention—are blocking me out, hoping to come up with the idea before I can market mine.

Gates: *(Nods slowly)* That's the way it is in some businesses. I've experienced it myself.

Annie: *(Proud of Jimmy)* It's a shame. It's a brilliant invention. *(Laughs)* Even I understand it, now that Jimmy has explained it to me for the last several months.

Jimmy: *(Happily)* But I can't tell you how much this check means to us. I'll go get that job, but now I can afford to be a bit choosy. That's a big help.

Gates: *(Takes out the paper, looks at it, shakes his head grimly, then suddenly grins and hands it to Jimmy)* Look at this.

Jimmy: *(Takes it and reads, slightly puzzled)* $75,000? *(Beat)* I don't understand.

Gates: *(Laughs)* Before you told me the figure you needed, I got a swift kick in the pants and it came to me. *(Nods at the paper)* I wrote that down BEFORE you said it aloud.

Jimmy: *(Nods, still puzzled)* Yes. I saw you do it. *(Beat)* But I still don't understand. *(A smile)* Except it means you're a great guesser or a mind reader.

Gates: *(Slowly shakes his head)* Neither. *(Looks at them carefully)* That's the amount of the legacy I mentioned before—AFTER taxes.

Annie: *(A wondering look)* Quite a coincidence.

Jimmy: *(Nods, smiles)* Incredible.

Gates: *(Shakes his head)* Don't you two know there are no coincidences like this when the Lord and His followers get together?

Jimmy: *(Deeper frown)* I still don't understand.

Gates: *(Grinning hugely)* Don't you?

Annie: *(Begins to cry, her face breaks out in a look of astonishment and awe)* You don't mean . . .

Gates: *(The big, big grin)* Like a partner, brother Jimmy?

Jimmy: *(Stares)* You mean—*(Gulps)* Are you serious?

Gates: *(Nods)* Yep. The kick in the pants did it. The Lord reminding me, I didn't earn that legacy. It was a gift. *(Nods smiling)* From an uncle I never met presumably. But we know where it really came from, don't we? *(Laughs)* I am just a steward of it—for a while. *(A Cheshire cat grin)* I have an idea that solar power system of yours is going to benefit a lot of people. *(Laughs)* After all, everybody needs the Son's power! *(The two of them stare at him and at each other and a tear or so runs down Annie's cheek. This time she hugs Jimmy and holds it for a long time. She's teared up pretty much, and even Jimmy has one or two of his own. They both, still with arms around each other, turn and look at Gates as though he were their brand new bouncing baby boy. He gets all embarrassed and looks down at his cake that now has a mysterious drop or two of some kind of water on it and gruffly)* For goodness' sake. *(Beat, the gruffness mixed with some humor)* EAT YOUR CAKE! *(There's a startled pause and then they all laugh. Gates starts eating and Annie and Jimmy hug each other and then dance about the room a bit. Gates looks on like an indulgent father. Music swells and the lights begin to dim to a blackout and curtain.)*

THE END

THE TIE THAT BINDS

Charles M. Tanner

CAST

Don Rowans...................A man with a problem—several actually.

Kerry Rowans................Don's wife. She shares Don's problem and has some of her own.

Barney Akers.................A very likable fellow. He considers Don and Kerry his best friends.

Debbie Strawn...............Engaged to Barney. This is her first visit to the Rowans's home.

Scene: This could be a living room or a den—even a patio—but it is where the activities of this family take place. It is about noon on a Saturday or Sunday. This is not a Christian family so Sunday means nothing to them. At CURTAIN, we see a man sitting slumped over in his chair. There is a cup of coffee on the table before him. He is moving as little as possible and is groaning, which sounds like a low chant. A few more beats and his wife comes in. She looks better but only by comparison. She moves silently to the table and pours herself a cup of coffee. We hear no sound but Don does. This is Don and Kerry Rowans.

Don: *(Shivering with hurt)* Shhhh. Not so loud.

Kerry: *(Flat)* I didn't say anything.

Don: *(Another shiver)* You made like Niagara Falls. Did you drop a bucket of water or something?

Kerry: *(Sarcastically)* I poured a cup of coffee. *(Beat)* A whole cup.

Don: *(Raises a feeble hand)* Don't pour cream in it. I couldn't stand it.

Kerry: *(Ignores him, pours the cream. He winces. She sits down noisily—to him, sips at the coffee)* You have a good time last night? *(She looks vaguely around the kitchen, could care less about his answer)*

Don: *(Fervently)* I hope so. The bill I'm paying this morning indicates I should have had a fantastic time.

Kerry: *(Sarcasm)* Let me be the first to inform you. You did have a fantastic time. *(Beat, dry)* At least you were fantastic. In the more revolting meaning of the word.

Don: *(Groans)* Oh, no.

Kerry: *(Happy to be squelching him)* Oh, yes. You were the life of the party. Never before had the assembled guests seen such a CLOWN act. I think they realized they were watching a real clown. Not an act.

Don: *(Sneers)* Happy birthday to you, too.

Kerry: *(Fast on him)* Speaking of that, I think your best bit was when you smothered yourself in the face with the whole cake. *(Sneers herself)* Everyone thought it was simply hilarious. *(Double beat)* Except the hostess. I don't think she thought it was so funny. *(Beat)* It being the only cake. *(Double beat)* And most of it ending up on—and in—the rug as you did your little Costello dance. *(Reaches over and taps him on the arm)* He did it better.

Don: *(Cringing)* Stop pounding me.

Kerry: *(A straight look)* I just tapped you. But I could be induced to pound with very little effort on your part.

Don: *(The hand waving again)* Don't pound.

Kerry: *(Sighs, sips)* One thing I'll say for you. We won't have to return their dinner invitation. *(Nods)* Quite understandably, they aren't speaking to us.

Don: *(Mumbles from under his arms)* I don't remember any of that.

Kerry: *(Sarcasm)* How's the sand in your nose?

Don: *(A small lift)* How'd I do that?

Kerry: *(Gestures at him)* You're doing it now. Ignoring the horrible things you have done on the premise that if you groan and whine and keep your eyes closed it will all go away. *(A beat and snappier)* Well, Emmett Kelly, it won't, but I think I will.

Don: *(Without looking up)* Go quietly.

Kerry: *(Angry, really angry)* Not likely! I intend to make all the noise I can packing.

Don: *(He groans, reaches for the coffee cup)* What packing?

Kerry: *(Coldly)* The things I'm taking with me, of course.

Don: *(Mutters)* Taking with you?

Kerry: Yeah. Taking with me. *(Beat)* Why don't you just think about it for a minute? Give those great, big words time to seep down through the sour mash fumes into what's left of your pickled brain.

Don: *(Noticing)* You're insulting me.

Kerry: See. Listen just a little and you'll get the drift of things.

Don: *(Rubs his head just a little)* My head hurts.

Kerry: *(Lightly)* Good. *(Sweet voice)* Anything I can do to make it worse?

Don: *(Shoves the cup at her)* Get me some coffee.

Kerry: *(Shrugs, gets up and does so)* Why not? One last act of married— whatever. *(Gets it, shoves it into his hand)*

Don: *(Pulls his hand away)* Ouch. That hurts.

Kerry: *(Nods)* That's nice. *(A small wave)* Well, so long, Charlie. *(Thinks hard)* But that's not your name, is it? *(Starts off)* Ah, how soon we forget. I'm forgetting you already. And I like it.

Don: *(Lifts his head a bit)* Where you going?

Kerry: *(Strikes a pose)* He's looking up. Maybe he—it is alive after all. *(Direct)* You still alive?

Don: *(Makes a face)* Barely. And you're not funny. Where are you going?

Kerry: *(Hands on hips)* I told you while you were out to lunch. That is, out to drink. *(A thought)* But that's okay—you drink your lunch, don't you?

Don: *(Squinting and making pained faces)* Tell me again. Where're you goin'?

Kerry: *(Succinctly and directly)* To pack.

Don: *(Groans)* Oh, no. Where're we going?

Kerry: *(Sarcasm)* WE are not going anywhere. YOU are going to slobber your life away on that table. I am leaving this house, the two cats, the mice your cats can't catch, and you. *(Beat)* Mostly you.

Don: *(Peers at her, twisted face)* You—are leaving me?

Kerry: *(Shakes her head)* Some brain left there, after all. *(Nods)* That's it, Herman. I am leaving you. *(Waves)* Bye.

Don: *(Quickly)* Wait a minute. *(He winces from the sound and movement)* Let's talk this over.

Kerry: *(Shrugs)* I've got five minutes more or less. Shoot. *(A tough smile)* Oh, what a lovely word.

Don: *(Puzzled)* You're leaving me because I got a little drunk last night?

Kerry: *(Hoots loudly)* A little drunk? You don't even know where you were last night.

Don: *(Hotly)* I was at a party.

Kerry: *(Leans toward him)* Where?

Don: *(Waves)* Somewhere. What's the difference? *(Stares at her)* I've got drunk before.

Kerry: *(Firmly)* You have indeed. You say that like it's some achievement.

Don: *(Shrugs)* Everybody drinks.

Kerry: *(Hard)* No, they don't. There is no law, and it doesn't take virility to lift a four-ounce glass and tumble some giggle juice down a throat.

Don: *(A shake)* Well, everybody drinks. You know what I mean.

Kerry: No, I don't. And not many can drink the way you do. You act like a camel after a week in the desert without a sip.

Don: *(Squints, ouch, it hurts, relaxes a bit)* Hey, you tryna make me out as an alcoholic? *(Snorts)* I'm no alcoholic.

Kerry: Uh huh. You know what is said, don't you?

Don: *(Waves again)* Yeah. Yeah, alkies never recognize they're alkies. But I don't drink that much.

Kerry: *(Paces angrily)* Oh, Don. You pour it down constantly. Is there a day you don't tilt the bottle?

Don: *(Trying to be funny)* Yeah. Some days I tilt a glass. *(He grins, horrible. And she marches rapidly for the door)* Hey, wait. So okay, it was a bum joke. I drink. Yeah, probably every day. But all the guys I know do it too.

Kerry: *(From near the door)* Maybe their wives are leaving them today also.

Don: *(A smile)* You're not going to leave me.

Kerry: *(Hard and meaning it)* I am going to leave you.

Don: *(A plea)* But we love each other.

Kerry: *(Flat)* We used to.

Don: *(Stares and begins to feel sorry for himself)* You mean you don't love me anymore.

Kerry: *(Shakes her head)* I don't love what you've become. I don't like what you've become.

Don: *(Deep frown)* Well, if I have become an alkie then don't you think a good wife would stay and help me lick it?

Kerry: We've been through that.

Don: *(Beginning to get worried)* We could try harder. I mean I would. *(A firm thought)* But I am not really an alcoholic—yet. I know inside I'm not. *(Shrugs)* I suppose I could—maybe will become one without some help. . . .

Kerry: *(Coldly)* Then you better go get it. There are places where you can get that kind of help. *(Hard)* Better than I can give you.

Don: *(Squinches up his face at her)* I can't believe you're going to leave me just because of last night.

Kerry: *(Sincerely)* It isn't because of last night. That was just the clincher. The snap I needed to get me over the hump of trying as hard as I could and snapping into the decision to call it quits. *(Leans again)* Don. *(Beat)* Quits. *(She starts out)*

Don: Wait, wait. Hold on. What else have I done that's so bad?

Kerry: *(Turns to him)* You're a flirt, Don. Old-fashioned word. It means you like to play dangerously. Do as much as you can. Get as far along as someone will let you without committing yourself. We don't have a proper word today for it. Sexual behavior is too cheap. There's no place for a middle-ground word.

Don: *(A beat)* I haven't had any affairs.

Kerry: *(Hard)* Not yet. But you're on the verge. You've been playing the cheap, low-cost, noncommitment game so long it's getting to be not enough anymore. *(Hard)* Isn't that right?

Don: *(Shrugs)* I don't know what you're talking about. *(Hard)* And I don't think you do, either. *(A side look)* You mean you haven't played those games, too?

Kerry: *(Shakes her head)* No. I'm not angelic, Don. There's very little reason to be these days. I haven't progressed beyond the early stages of victorian flirting.

Don: *(Tries to be sarcastic, can't handle it well)* Oh really?

Kerry: *(Evenly)* Yes. Really. *(Looks off)* If I stay married to you—as we are now—I'll get there. It's the natural flow of the stream we wiggle around in. *(To him, hurting)* But I don't like that sordid world and I'm getting out when I can.

Don: *(Snaps)* You think you can find some place where they don't play these games?

Kerry: *(Explosive positiveness)* Oh, absolutely. Most of the people in this country are above these sneak-around-the-back-of-the-barn childishnesses.

Don: *(Looks away)* I don't mean anything by it. None of it means anything.

Kerry: *(Is that a tear in her eye)* It does to me. It means a great deal. Along with everything else it's too much to handle. *(There's a knock on the door and then a breezy . . .)*

Barney: *(Barney Akers comes happily in, big smiles)* Hi, you two. *(Sees Don)* Oh, oh. *(Beat)* You been in an accident? *(Without waiting for an answer)* Hey, look at this exquisite woman. *(He points out Debbie Strawn)* We're thinking of getting married.

Don: *(Mutters sourly)* Good idea. Keep thinking about it for about ten years and then forget it.

Kerry: *(Flat)* Paraphrasing Mark Twain. *(To Don)* Didn't know you'd read him. *(Double beat)* Didn't know you read.

Barney: *(Alarmed)* Uh, oh. A fight. Hey, you two don't fight. You're not allowed to. Not on the day that this lovely, slightly demented creature and I am—*(makes a face)* are—never can figure that out right. In any case—getting married.

Kerry: *(Sighs)* You picked a bad time, Barney. *(Hand out)* Anyway, hi, I'm Kerry.

Debbie: *(Alert but seeks to overlook)* Hi. Barney talks about you two all the time.

Barney: *(Proudly)* And not just because they owe me money, either. *(A wave and a grin)* They're my best friends. They're married.

Kerry: *(Murmurs)* Momentarily.

Barney: *(Stares at her)* Huh?

Don: *(Getting up and reeling a bit, ooooooh that hurts)* She's just kidding.

Kerry: *(Flat)* She's not kidding.

Barney: *(Stares)* You're not kidding?

Don: *(Nods)* Yes, she is.

Kerry: *(Firmly)* No, I'm not.

Debbie: *(Pulling at Barney's sleeve)* I think we should leave. *(Brightly)* We have so much to do.

Barney: *(To her, a plea)* Hey, I can't leave my best friends just when they need me.

Kerry: *(Pushes at him with a smile)* We don't need you. Run along. *(A grimace)* Sorry, Debbie.

Debbie: *(Thoughtfully)* That's all right. *(A beat)* Could Barney help? I'm all for it if he could.

Don: *(Waves)* Aw, what can he do? *(Waves at her)* She's made up her mind. She thinks I'm an alcoholic.

Kerry: *(Hard at him)* I didn't say THAT. I said you drink too much and you drink all the time.

Don: *(A gesture to them)* See?

Barney: *(Evenly)* Hey, old buddy, don't look at me. I think you drink too much. And I've told you so.

Debbie: *(Uneasily)* I don't think that's helping, Barney.

Don: *(Hard at Barney)* No, it's not.

Barney: *(A wave back at Don)* Hey, we're better friends than that. I don't have to agree with you for us to be friends. You DO drink too much.

Don: *(Upset with everything at this point)* So okay. Maybe she burns the bacon.

Kerry: *(A straight look at Don)* Yes. Maybe I do. Or some other such crime. *(Softer)* I am not trying to put the blame on you for our separation, Don. I spoke of drink because you wanted to know why. That's one of the whys.

Barney: *(Nods)* There, Don, she's not blaming you for everything. So stop fighting. While you're at it—stop drinking. *(He grins)* I'm being funny.

Don: *(Sharply)* Don't think so. *(To Kerry)* We gonna discuss the family faults in front of these people?

Kerry: *(Starts out again)* No. We aren't going to discuss the family faults at all. *(Quieter)* I'm just leaving.

Debbie: *(Taps Barney)* Come on, Barney.

Kerry: *(To her)* No, no, stay. I've got to pack and I would rather that Don wasn't all over the room discussing the family faults while I do. Keep him company.

Don: *(Sees he'd better get off his angry horse. Kerry is now determined.)* All right, all right, just a minute. *(Tosses his arms out)* What *can* we do? I don't want a divorce. I'll admit there's something wrong with the marriage. I don't think it's drink. Not at the bottom, but I'll come to some terms with you about that.

Barney: *(Earnestly)* If that isn't the bottom line, what do you think is, Don?

Don: *(Glumly)* I don't know.

Kerry: *(Softer, sighing)* I think I do. But in general terms. The tie that binds. *(Beat)* We don't have one. We don't have anything so powerful, so strong, so natural to each of us and enjoined to the both of us that it would hold us together during crises—major and minor.

Debbie: *(Nods)* That sounds very clear. Very important.

Barney: *(Nods)* Yeah, *(looks at Debbie)* A good thing to know. And remember.

Don: *(Thinks hard)* Well . . . we got as much as we ever had, don't we?

Kerry: *(Shrugs)* I don't know. I don't think so. I think we lost something somewhere—but I can't put my finger on it.

Don: *(Shrugs)* Well, I suppose I'm not as romantic as I was when we were first married, but then no man can stay that way.

Debbie: *(A look at Barney)* Is that so? Maybe I shall be learning something, too.

Barney: *(Fast)* Hey, wait a minute. This guy is my best friend, but that doesn't mean he has to make sense when he speaks. *(To Don, disgustedly)* Man, you don't make sense.

Don: *(A wave)* Wait'll you're married for a while. You'll find out.

Barney: *(Hotly to him)* Look, Don, my parents have been married a lot longer than you—about ten times more, I'd guess—and my Dad is still romantic with Mom. He brings her things—often—right out of the blue. Does special little things for her when she least expects it. He's not afraid to tell her that he loves her either. *(Beat)* And I suppose you'd think he was an old man.

Don: *(Stares at him)* No, I don't think your father is an old man. *(Beat)* Does he really—do all—that—stuff?

Barney: *(Mimicking him)* Yes, he does do all that stuff.

Debbie: *(Big smile)* And you paid attention and learned from him, Barney?

Barney: *(Grins at her)* Yes. I did. *(A loving smile)* And I promise I will always follow his example.

Don: *(Stares at them grinning at each other and then stares at Kerry)* Is that what you want?

Kerry: *(Aloof)* It would have helped.

Don: *(Shrugs, makes a face)* I suppose I could give it a try.

Kerry: *(Shakes her head)* Not good enough, Don. Not nearly good enough. Supposing you could make a try—that line is a built-in preparation for defeat. And it's not going to be mine.

Don: *(A cry, too much complaining in the tone)* What do you want from me?

Kerry: *(Cool now)* A divorce. That's all.

Barney: *(Bustling with energy)* No, no. No you don't. Hold on. You don't really want a divorce. And since you don't down deep, let's work it over some more.

Kerry: *(Shakes her head)* I don't WANT a divorce deep down inside . . . of course not. I don't want one even on a more superficial level than that. *(A deep feeling)* But I see no other alternative. We have no real thread to bind us together. Nothing substantial—real. Something stronger than we are even, so we won't break it out of sheer thrashing about or innate perversity.

Debbie: *(Nods)* I see what you mean.

Barney: *(Earnestly)* But then you must find something. There's got to be something you could both agree upon and find strong enough to do the job.

Kerry: *(Wearily again)* What for instance?

Barney: *(Stares back at her)* It would take—working out. If you only worked together, that might do it.

Don: *(A tad flip)* I could quit my job, and we could start up a cottage industry of some kind.

Kerry: *(Patting Barney's arm, preparing to leave)* Thanks for your help, Barney.

Don: *(Fast)* Come on, Kerry, you know that I always get flip when I'm nervous and worried. I don't want a divorce. I honestly don't. And that makes me very nervous indeed.

Kerry: *(Sighs)* I know. But it will still be the best for both of us in the long run.

Don: I don't think so.

Debbie: *(Shakes her head)* I see her point. Two people do need a tie of strong binding to make a marriage last and last AS BRIGHT AS WHEN IT BEGAN.

Barney: *(Chewing his lip)* Uh huh. For Mom and Dad it is the Lord of course.

Debbie: *(With a hidden meaning in her voice)* I know.

Don: *(Shrugs)* You gotta believe all that first. Who can?

Barney: *(Looks off)* Well. *(Thinks better of what he was going to say)* For Debbie and me, it's a crazy love of travel. *(Proudly)* We both got jobs on a cruise liner. She a photographer and me an editorialist. *(Laughs)* Writer of everything. Ship's paper, menus, bulletins, the works. *(Grins, takes her arm)* That's what holds us together, isn't that right, Debbie?

Debbie: *(Smiles at him, she has a plan)* We'll see.

Kerry: *(Looks down at her shoes)* The Lord. Church. *(To Don)* Funny, isn't it? That's where we met. At Church.

Debbie: *(To Barney, whispers in his ear and they slip out quietly after Barney stares at Kerry and Don and sees how they are looking at each other. Kerry and Don don't notice. Barney is always in and out)*

Don: *(Getting a more lively look on his face)* Yeah. That's right. I'd almost forgotten. *(Looks off)* That's when I was going . . .

Kerry: *(Another look down)* You were always so dead set against Christianity, I'd never pushed but . . .

Don: *(Looks off, too)* Never told you. A chaplain in college. He was found to have been playing games with coeds. A big scandal. He ended up in more trouble than he could handle. He committed suicide. And he was an ordained minister. *(Mumbles)* Also a guy I looked up to.

Kerry: *(Stares at him)* And you blamed Christianity for that? You blamed Jesus for this man's behavior?

Don: *(Surprised at her vehemence)* Well. . . . I was young I guess, and it did seem that if this is the way church leaders acted I wanted no part of it.

Kerry: *(Shakes her head in frustration)* And so you DID put all the onus on Christ. Made him the scapegoat once again.

Don: *(Stares at her)* You? You are—interested—in church?

Kerry: *(Firmly)* In Christianity. Yes. But I didn't say anything because I wanted *(now she runs down as she sees how dumb THIS point is)* . . . to make our marriage go. *(Stares off, mouth open)* I just realized I did the same thing. Our next door neighbor where I grew up, pressured her husband something awful about going to church, and one day he just up and left. She never saw him again. *(Stares and shakes her head and paces)* That's what I was afraid of—losing the marriage if I tried to force you to attend church. *(Beat as she thinks about this, thunderstruck)* So we just—didn't go.

Don: *(Sees hope)* Look, Kerry, maybe that would work. I mean we could find a church—start going. Maybe that would be this tie you're talking about. What do you think?

Kerry: *(Looks at him. She does love him, but she is aware how easy things don't work)* Maybe, Don. There might be a chance. But not the easy way. We'd just forget this day and what'd transpired and go our same old way again. *(Gently)* I am going to leave. But a separation, not a complete cut-off. *(Holds her hands up)* No. No more discussion. I am convinced this is best. I'll call you when I get located. Don't worry about me. I'll be all right. *(A beat)* Then you can call me if you like. If you want to keep this marriage, you are going to have to court me again. Another old-fashioned word—COURT. Nice one though. It will teach us both about the reality of romance. As opposed to sentimentality. *(Starts for the door)* I, for one, am starting to go to church. I want to find HIM. *(Gentler still)* I think, if you really want our marriage to continue, you had better search HIM out, too. *(At the door)* Stay where you are, Don. I'll pack and leave. You remain here. We are going to do this the hard way. *(Smiles)* I think that's the only way that ever works.

Don: *(Nods)* All right, Kerry. We'll work at it together. The hard way. And my drinking too.

Kerry: *(Smiles)* I think if you find HIM, He'll take care of that for you. IF you work at it. *(Points to him)* Stay there. *(A nice smile)* I DO love you.

Don: *(A nice smile)* And I DO love you.

(She turns and hurries through the door to cover the tears that come, and Don sits back down. Tight, nervous, but determined to learn a lesson, a permanent lesson about love, marriage, and "The Tie That Binds." DIM to BLACKOUT and CURTAIN slowly closes as he—son of a gun—might remember praying.)

THE END

IF YOU DON'T LIKE THE FACTS, CHANGE THEM

Charles M. Tanner

CAST

Mrs. Black.............A very important community observer. Just ask her.

Mrs. Gray ....The willing audience for Mrs. Black.

John ....A high placed and trusted executive.

Harry....................Also an executive—and a deal-maker.

Delcie ....A professional who is a committed Christian.

Jezzie ....Friend of Delcie's, also a professional. She's on a campaign.

Optional Extras ....Waitresses, other customers

Scene: This takes place at a coffee shop—any kind will do. Several tables (at least three), chairs, a serving counter. The usual commercial pictures on the walls, perhaps a plant or two for decoration, the coffee pot on the warmer, and whatever else will augment and support. At CURTAIN we see two of the tables with people. At Table # 1 are Mrs. Black and Mrs. Gray, and at Table # 2 are John and Harry. Each are tightly in their own conversation. The volume comes up first for us on Table # 1.

Mrs. Black: *(Leans toward the other)* You remember Grace Stevens? *(Moves right on)* Welllllll. What I heard about her . . .

Mrs. Gray: *(Anxiously waits and then prods the other)* Yes, yes. What did you hear?

Mrs. Black: *(Takes a deep breath)* Well, I suppose I shouldn't say anything. *(Pompously)* I am not, after all, a gossip!

Mrs. Gray: *(Knowing this is merely a preamble)* Of course not. *(Fast and eager)* What did you hear?

Mrs. Black: *(Continues rapidly, naturally)* Welllllllll, Janie Dumont told me, and you know she'll tell anything, but this is—welllll, VEREEEEEE interesting.

Mrs. Gray: *(Nudges her a bit)* Well, for heaven's sakes, stop beating around the bush and tell me. Tell me! You know I won't tell anyone.

Mrs. Black: *(Licks her lips)* All right. But don't tell anyone. I DID tell Janie I wouldn't say a word. *(Archly)* But after all . . . to you. . . . *(The volume drops and Mrs. Black and Mrs. Gray exit deeply engrossed in their conversation. The volume immediately comes up for us on Table #2.)*

John:	*(Begins talking in audible tones, obviously in the middle of a conversation)* I've got the specs right here, but they're still so secret I had to sneak them out of the office.
Harry:	*(Coldly)* I don't buy unless I know something. The inside. The things others don't know.
John:	*(Nods)* I know that. That's why I've got the dope with me. But you've got to promise not to divulge the information to anyone.
Harry:	*(Easily)* Sure. In business you've got to have a trust factor.
John:	*(Nods)* And I have a high one at my company. *(Beat)* That's why I had to sneak this volatile stuff out.
Harry:	*(Understands)* Okay. Shoot.
John:	*(Looks around)* There's something here that'll curl your hair. *(John and Harry drop their volume and prepare to leave just as Dulcie and Jezzie work their way to the down-stage table. John and Harry exit upper stage still dealing.)*
Delcie:	*(Grins)* What're you doing, Jezzie? Running for some office or other? *(Looks about, gesturing)* I see you buttonholing people all over. *(Laughs)* Now me. *(Beat)* Want my vote for something?
Jezzie:	*(Nods, eager and driving)* Yes, I guess I do, but I hadn't thought of it—like that.
Delcie:	*(Laughs again)* You want my vote but hadn't thought of it—like that. You fascinate me. Sell away.
Jezzie:	*(Fast)* Well, I'm not actually selling, but I am trying to get people together.
Delcie:	*(Hands in the air, knowing that this is not it)* A party. Yeah!
Jezzie:	*(Shakes her head)* No. It's not a party. Look. It's about church. I have been—
Delcie:	*(Delighted)* Jezzie! You're getting interested in the church? How wonderful!
Jezzie:	*(Makes a face)* No, no, not like that. I have been going to quite a few churches lately and I can't find any that satisfy me . . . suit me . . . if you know what I mean.

Delcie: *(Slumps a little)* I'm afraid I do.

Jezzie: *(Defensively)* The churches—all I've attended—every one of them keeps trying to put me down and I'm getting tired of it. Tired and determined to do something about it.

Delcie: *(Quick recover)* Good. *(Beat)* You're going to start a reformation in one or another of them?

Jezzie: *(Waves that off)* Well, I may start a reformation but it won't be in any of the churches that are in operation now.

Delcie: *(Stunned a bit)* You're going to start a new church?

Jezzie: *(Nods)* That's right. I'm in the process right now.

Delcie: *(Startled)* But Jezzie, you aren't ordained. *(Beat)* I don't mean to hurt, but you haven't even seemed interested in—well the Bible, theology, the Christian demands—

Jezzie: *(Cutting in)* That's it. You've hit the nail on the head. Demands! *(Angrily)* I'm tired of demands. I'm tired of the church pounding at YOU about being somebody different following all those rules, changing your lives, becoming mice instead of people.

Delcie: *(The truth)* You stun me.

Jezzie: *(Happily)* Good. Listen, I'm forming the Society of Unlimited Nominal Christians. *(Fast)* We're going to have our own church and believe me, it will be a comfortable place to come to, a haven, a sanctuary, a—

Delcie: *(Shocked again)* A sanctuary!

Jezzie: *(Fast)* Oh, not the way you mean the word. But a place to escape all the criticisms, the guilt complexes, the worrying about—*(Makes an awful face)* sin. Ughhhh.

Delcie: *(Double meaning)* You don't like sin?

Jezzie: *(Hard)* I sure don't, I'm tired—

Delcie: *(Nods)* That's good, Jezzie. God doesn't either.

Jezzie: *(Hoots)* God doesn't! How many times have I heard that. No that's not what I mean. I mean I don't like HEARING about it all the time. That's old-fashioned stuff that has no place in our modern world.

Delcie:	*(Fast)* I agree. There's no place for sin in this modern world.
Jezzie:	*(Harder)* Oh stop preaching at me and listen. You said you would.
Delcie:	*(A thought)* I don't think I said exactly that, but go ahead. I'll try to be— quiet.
Jezzie:	*(Snorts)* Sin! Now what kind of a word is that? I'll tell you. It's a word designed to make everyone fill with fear so the church will have a hold over you. That's all. They've taken everything that is fun and pleasurable and made a sin out of it. That way you are more willing to do whatever they want so they'll remove that terrible feeling from you.
Delcie:	*(Mildly)* You don't think that secular people feel the guilt of sin?
Jezzie:	*(Hard)* If they do, it is because of the church's influence. That's all.
Delcie:	*(Still mild)* Well, I'm glad the church DOES have some influence.
Jezzie:	*(Pushing her point)* You see, the church pounds at us all the time. Commitments, for instance. They're always harping on commitment. Meaning that they want you to be sure to be at their beck and call, obeying their rules all the time.
Delcie:	*(Gently)* Commitment is basically to Jesus Christ—to God—isn't it?
Jezzie:	*(Waves this away as if it is mere camouflage)* You gotta commit, and then they expect you to KEEP that commitment even when you have a BETTER idea. A better thought and like that.
Delcie:	*(Can't believe this)* Incredible.
Jezzie:	*(Throws her arms into the air)* And finances! Welllll, what can I or anyone say? They just want your money. Or worse, they want you to work for the church—
Delcie:	*(Gently cutting in)* Christianity.
Jezzie:	*(Stubbornly)* The church wants you to work for nothing, or for very low pay. And they expect you to be happy about it. *(Angrily)* It makes me mad whenever ANYONE works hard for the church without getting paid good money. *(Explaining)* That makes me feel guilty you see because I may not be doing that. And I don't like feeling guilty.
Delcie:	*(Nods)* Yes. I'm getting that impression.

Jezzie: *(Waxing enthusiastic)* Always after money, the church is. Revamping, expanding, extending, keeping other people going somewhere *(gestures vaguely)* way off someplace. New projects—they're never satisfied with the old ones they're embroiled in. Missionaries! Missionaries! Don't they know the times have passed for that kind of stuff? Leave people alone, that's my motto. Let people be what they want to be.

Delcie: *(Evenly)* Suppose they aren't anything?

Jezzie: *(Fast)* Then let them be—nothing. That's their business. Missionaries are always muddling around. Trying to bring Jesus into EVERYBODY'S lives!

Delcie: *(Nods)* You don't believe in Jesus then. Or God, I suppose?

Jezzie: *(Hard and a bit miffed)* Of course I believe in God. In Jesus. *(Frowns)* That's why the word *Christian* is in our group's name. I just don't believe in being maniacal about it. I don't want to be told about sin, or to give more and more money. And I don't want to have drummed into my head every time I turn around about things like commitment, duty, obedience, rules, rules, rules! I want—and plan—to be a Christian—the easy way. I don't want constantly to be disturbed—hounded—pummeled— admonished—corrected—criticized and challenged. *(Beat)* I'll, uh, challenge myself. *(Beat)* If it is ever necessary.

Delcie: *(A small smile)* I can see where it probably won't be necessary.

Jezzie: *(Nods easily)* Probably not. *(Fast)* I mean, God is not an ogre. He's not going to clobber me because I do a few of what the church keeps calling sins. *(Spits it out)* Sins.

Delcie: *(Frowns—mock)* Hmmmm. It seems to me that the Bible calls them sins. Did so first.

Jezzie: *(Laughs)* Yeah, come on, Delcie, the Bible is a great book but it was written thousands of years ago and can hardly be considered a treatise on modern behavior patterns. Really.

Delcie: *(Stares)* You don't believe the Bible is the basis for all Christian—uh *(Looks off)* you don't like the word BEHAVIOR. Let's see? *(Half beat)* How about—WALK? The Christian walk?

Jezzie: *(Fast)* Of course it is, but you have to do some selecting. Lots of things are just plain inapplicable. They don't—*(grins)* compute.

Delcie: *(Pulling her leg)* Of course, God wouldn't have a computer.

Jezzie: *(Easily)* I don't know if He has one or not. But the point is, we do. It's a modern, technological world and must have a proper technological philosophy. *(Nods thoughtfully)* As long as Christianity can be adaptable to that modern philosophy, then it has a place.

Delcie: *(Evenly)* I'm so glad.

Jezzie: *(Persuasively)* I believe I'm making progress with you. Now —

Delcie: *(Startled)* You do?

Jezzie: *(Smiles fatuously)* Yes. Now, just keep an open mind here. There's one more thing I can't stand and absolutely don't believe in. *(Beat)* Judgment! *(Laughs)* No, Delcie, come on, be reasonable, how could any of us face judgment if the Bible were to be taken as a factual book? How? Really.

Delcie: *(Smiles warmly)* We could not, of course, Jezzie.

Jezzie: *(Happily)* You see? You are listening. I knew you would.

Delcie: *(Speaking slowly as though to explain to someone who is thick)* We could not stand up to judgment—none of us. That is perfectly clear and true. Not by ourselves. BUT, Jezzie! We do not stand in judgment alone. Jesus the Christ will be there. Defending us with the total power of GRACE, which alone is enough to acquit us FOREVER. *(Smiles)* For when we look up at the Judge—it will be the same Jesus, the Christ, who has defended us and will absolve us by that Grace.

Jessie: *(Snorts)* Nice statement. Pretty and all wrapped up. But as I see it, the church insists there is to be Judgment and that all will stand before it — guilty.

Delcie: *(A plea)* But don't you see—

Jezzie: *(Cutting in)* I see only that it would be impossible. Positively impossible. And *(beat)* so I don't believe in it. No one could.

Delcie: *(Nods)* I do. And—because of the resurrection—I am not afraid of it, either.

Jezzie: *(Waves it away)* You're like so many others—too stubborn to listen. *(Hard)* Well, we do have many adherents and will do all right, thank you. *(Firmly)* The church is too hard. The Bible is too hard. *(A shrug)* Without some judicious editing.

Delcie: *(Nodding)* And, of course, Christianity is too hard, too.

Jezzie: *(Shakes her head)* No, no. It doesn't have to be. We'll have a church, you see, and it'll be a relaxed place where everyone can find a sanctuary against sin and judgment.

Delcie: *(Nods, smiles)* Good. I mean, good that it will be a sanctuary against sin and judgment.

Jezzie: *(Irritated)* No! I mean no, no. Not that way. We shall be safe from it because we shall—ignore it. It will just simply—cease to exist.

Delcie: *(Gently)* Eternally?

Jezzie: *(Stares at her, a quizzical look)* Yes. Yes, it will because those things can't exist for human beings. That's all. Positive and period.

Delcie: *(Looks away, sadly)* Period. An end.

Jezzie: *(Not understanding)* Right. An end to all the pressure and the demands. *(Sighs heavily)* Well, I can see you are too stubborn to listen to reason.

Delcie: *(Nods, gets up)* Yes, I probably am too stubborn to listen to a siren song that has no meaning—no reason—to me. *(Heads toward the door)* I wonder if you pray? If you will pray—at all. *(At the door)* I will. *(Smiles sadly at her)* For you and your adherents. *(Starts out, turns back)* Society of Unlimited Nominal Christians. *(A strong, steady gaze)* Interesting initials, don't you thing? *(Half beat)* S U N C! (Pronounced "sunk," of course. *And she exits leaving a puzzled and still disturbed Jezzie staring after her.)*

THE END